Wakefield Press

Preparing for Business

Geoff Goodfellow has lived and worked as a full time poet for 37 years. He has travelled extensively, performing nationally and internationally, sharing the stage with luminaries such as Ken Kesey.

Geoff is a confronting performer of his gutsy, colloquial, but also humorous poetry. He doesn't write to necessarily make readers feel comfortable, but rather, at times, to make them wriggle and squirm. Many of his poems will take his readers into territory where they might not, generally, venture.

Geoff Goodfellow's *Poems for a Dead Father* was shortlisted for the *Age* Book of the Year. His prose memoir, *Out of Copley Street: A working class boyhood*, revealing his early life in the inner-northern suburbs of Adelaide was published in late 2020 by Wakefield Press.

T0362939

Also by Geoff Goodfellow

Poetry

No Collars No Cuffs

Bow Tie & Tails

No Ticket No Start: Poetry from the building sites

Triggers: Turning experiences into poetry

Triggers: the video

The Sex Poems Unleashed

Semi Madness: Voices from Semaphore

Love is Cruel

Love is Cruel: Spoken word + music CD

Poems for a Dead Father

*Punch On Punch Off: poems for the employed, unemployed
and under-employed*

Waltzing with Jack Dancer: A slow dance with cancer

Opening the Windows to Catch the Sea Breeze: Selected poems 1983–2011

The People's Poet Transformed

(with Rebecca Bond)

Prose

Out of Copley Street: A working-class boyhood

PREPARING FOR BUSINESS
GEOFF GOODFELLOW

Wakefield Press

Wakefield Press
16 Rose Street
Mile End
South Australia 5031
www.wakefieldpress.com.au

First published 2021

Cover designed by Simon Cecere
Cover photograph by Simon Cecere
Typeset by Michael Deves, Wakefield Press

ISBN 978 1 74305 811 4

NATIONAL
LIBRARY
OF AUSTRALIA

A catalogue record for this
book is available from the
National Library of Australia

For my children
Mark, Shane, Paul and Grace
and my grandchildren
Della, Riley, Mason, Lilli and Healey

Contents

Kapok Pillow

Dad was one of the 'Rats of Tobruk'
    & at home during my early
childhood
    we often had our own private
theatre of war

dad going awol from work
    drinking the day away . . .
to stagger home mid-afternoon
& throw missiles around
    barking orders like the
RSM he never was

if we were lucky he might just
fall into bed
    still in his y-fronts & singlet
& far too drunk to reach his socks
    he'd gradually fill the ashtray
on his bedside table
    & if luck stayed with us –
he'd likely go off on the nod

i remember lifting a red brick
alongside the veranda
one hot summer's day after school
    & grabbing our front door key

there was a strange smell when i
let myself in
    a smell i couldn't recognise –
& i panicked

i tip-toed through the hallway slowly ...
    checked the kitchen & the laundry
looking for mum   then the clothes line –
    but she didn't seem to be
anywhere

i kept sniffing the air
    calling softly in my little boy's voice
mum   mum   are you there

yet nothing came back but a smell
    which i could only sense as death

after weeks of dad's drinking
    & arguments
    & threats
    & broken crockery
& living with the fear
    i inched my way along
the passage
    sniffing the acrid air ...
& when i got to the toilet
    the door was flung wide open
& the white porcelain pan was
choked high above the wooden
seat with a charry mess

it gave off the smell of death
& i looked around for an axe
　　i thought it was my mother's
torso

my tears & wails brought him
out of the bedroom
　　unsteady in his grey socks
he slurred
　　ya mum's out shopping
don't worry about that mess –
i went to sleep with a cigarette
　　i stuffed me pillow down
the toilet & pulled the chain
　　it's gone out now . . .
ya mother'll be in soon
　　go outside & get some fresh air
go on

& he turned on his heels
　　& staggered back to bed.

Rats of Tobruk: The name given to the predominantly
Australian soldiers of the garrison who held the Libyan
port of Tobruk against the Afrika Corps, during the siege
of Tobruk in WW2.

RSM: Regimental Sergeant Major

Snowboots

My state school education
started with Mister Keen
in '57
    standing over me
with an RSL badge pinned
to his wide lapel
    i was captured
in a steel-framed chair

KEEN he roared
& DON'T YOU FORGET IT –
K – DOUBLE E – N
    SAME AS THE MUSTARD
BUT TWICE AS HOT
    & ANYONE WHO CHALLENGES ME
WILL FIND THAT OUT

later he told us how he'd been
challenged in the Western Desert
    & how the Eyeties waved
a white flag
    & then he reckoned
that with some of our fathers
    he'd driven the Krauts
right back

life seemed serious in the suburbs
then
    but he liked a good laugh too

& showed it the morning Werner
arrived in lederhosen
    we tagged him *Hitler & The Hun*
& he'd always join in
when boys named Jan arrived

but it's a desert day in Adelaide
that i remember best
    i spotted Pellegrini
tramping through molten bitumen
in fur-lined boots
    i nicknamed him Snowboots
then–
    & it stuck on everyone's tongue
for the next five years

& five is what you'd likely get for
manslaughter

but Pellegrini's been sentenced
again
    given ten with no parole –
a psych report located an IQ of 74
& said he was disturbed
    & he was –
by a housewife returning home

so disturbed
    he buried her with his blade.

Copley Street

It was summer of 1960 & i was
twelve years of age
    World War 2 had finished
fifteen years earlier
    yet there was still fighting
going on in my street

i'd just been through a winter
cutting firewood armed with
a crosscut saw
    & i'd learnt how to swing
an axe
    & my biceps & shoulders
proved it

one afternoon a boy who lived
nine houses away
    wrapped a whip he'd made
from five strand electrical cord
around my arm

after i unwound it i ran home
& went through the backdoor crying

my old man was half drunk & didn't
want to hear how this boy was
older and taller
    get out there & give him a hiding –

you don't run away
    you don't squib it

two nights later i found the boy in
the street
    i belted him to the ground
& punched him senseless
    only letting go when someone
else's father stepped in & dragged
me off

leave me alone & mind y'r own
business   i screamed
    & he slunk off down his
driveway   hands on hips –
telling me i was *a little hooligan*
    while Michael ran for home

the following Sunday morning
i was walking home from the deli
smoking a Viscount Red
    when Michael's father spotted me
& drew his car to a halt

it was a brand new 1960 Holden Special
    white with a tan flash
& it was gleaming
    he jumped out & pointed his index
finger at me like it was a gun & started
ranting about how i'd belted his son
& how it better not happen again

i stubbed my cigarette out into the
unmade road & moved in on him
till we were eyeball to eyeball
　　i told him to get back into his car
or i'd give him what i'd given his son
surprisingly
　　he did as he was told
then drove away slowly . . .
　　yelling out all sorts of things

is it ever too late　　to apologise.

Even Now

It was 1961 & i was hovering
on thirteen years of age

i was less than a mile from the
starkness of my own street with
its unmade road
    ambling along Galway Avenue –
mid-afternoon
    the sun warming my back . . .
filtered light flecking the footpath
through the white cedars
    & young saplings reaching up
from the wide median strip
alive with the sounds of native birds

it was then i first saw Roslyn

she was twelve & a half   wore pigtails
tied with blue ribbon
    & a check dress that sat high
above her knees

i don't know how i found the courage
to chat her up
    i think i began by commenting
on how tiny her freckles were to mine
    but maybe i'm just imagining that . . .
hell   this was over fifty years ago

we were standing in dappled shade
    a stone's throw from Mrs Day's
kindergarten   so maybe i'd asked
if she'd gone there too

after five minutes of small talk
    all the while both of us moving
from foot to foot
    i began to make a move . . .
& in hindsight   so did she

we took off hand-in-hand retracing
her steps
    looking for somewhere private

i wanted to kiss her
    & i'd made my intentions clear

i hadn't kissed a girl before

at the time i shared a bedroom
with two younger brothers
    & when i knew i was alone . . .
i'd practise on the dressing table
mirror   always careful to wipe away
any evidence

at the end of Collingrove Ave we came
across a red brick Baptist Church
    & on the side   a small porch –
its white wooden doors   unlocked

once inside   my hands were full
of her   & hers   with me –
& when our wet tongues touched
　　i felt my knees begin to buckle

maybe i became too big for my britches
　　anyway –
i must have scared her because she
pulled away & stuttered she had to go
　　yet promised she'd meet me
the following day at four o'clock

& even now   each time i pass that
red brick church   i keep an eye out
for her
　　just as i did that following day

& even now   when i do think of her
　　my breath quickens.

First Flush

Like many boys at thirteen i was
obsessed with sex
        stick books lined the bottom
of my kit bag while testosterone
dripped out of my body twenty-
four seven   like the leaking tap
at the bottom of our garden

each night i'd roll around alone
in my single bed
        trying to divert my amorous
thoughts by reciting Pythagoras's
Theorem   or i'd learn by rote
lines from a John Masefield poem
        or perhaps Wordsworth
or even Longfellow
        but some nights the mere
thought of Longfellow would
send me off to thoughts of sex
        & i'd conjure up the lanky girl
with the ponytail who'd served me
from behind the checkout at Woolies
        & what we might do together
when the store closed

other nights it might be the girl
behind the counter at the chemist
shop who'd know where the frangers
were kept

& i'd wonder if i'd ever get
brave enough to ask for a packet
of three   & if i did . . .
would she blush too   or would she say
   we've also got packets of twelve

& what would i say then

but more often than not i'd conjure up
an image of that older woman who
took me by surprise as i was dropping
off two pints of milk on the run one
morning   how she opened up the
front door around 6:30 one chilly autumn
morning as i placed those clinking
bottles in her wire carrier
   then rattled me when she suddenly
stepped out barefoot onto that
cold concrete veranda
   her red painted toenails almost
glowing   & when i looked up our
eyes met momentarily & then mine fell
lazily down her body
   her translucent pink nylon nightie
was all that separated us   apart from
about twenty years
   & i knew she saw my eyes travel
& gleam as i surveyed her near
nakedness   & even now i can still
remember the cup of her breasts
   the protrusion of her nipples

& the look of that soft fur that i longed
to stroke

but i was scared too that she was
going to invite me inside
        i knew her husband would then
be able to read my mind
        & i ran back to the horse & cart
flushed with embarrassment
        & far too fearful to look back
as much as i wanted to

it took another three years before
a girl older & far more experienced
than me took me mid-winter on the
cold vinyl backseat of a Holden Special
late one evening   the frosted windows
where we had earlier written *FOREVER*
        & drawn love hearts & arrows
& our initials with our wet fingertips
        both of us knowing nothing ...
but that night thinking we owned
the world & each other
        & all that i had been dreaming of
& planning & scheming for the past
three years
        took fully three minutes to execute

& even that
        is perhaps a gross exaggeration.

Understanding It

At the age of thirteen
i was smoking 2 ounces of Drum
　　each & every week

at the age of thirteen
i was able to unclip a bra
　　single-handedly

at the age of thirteen
i could do fifty push-ups
　　& a hundred sit-ups

at the age of thirteen
i'd been refused re-enrolment
　　at a technical high school

at the age of thirteen
i thought i was fully formed
　　& invincible

now at seventy after surviving
cancer & two failed marriages
　　i'm beginning to understand.

Flexing Muscles

Dad's elbows were resting
on the kitchen table
    the *Advertiser* stretched out
in front of him & he was mumbling
about the threat of a nuclear war

it was October of 1962
    & Khrushchev & Castro were
flexing their muscles at JFK

i was flexing my own
    standing in front of dad's shaving
mirror wearing my new black shirt
    the sleeves rolled up tight
against my now bulging biceps

there won't be a war i said
    you carry on about that
all the time

his blue eyes came up over his horn rim
glasses & he stared me down
    don't be so bloody sure about
that   & what are you doing flexing
your muscles

i might get a tattoo   i told him

don't be so bloody stupid
     you won't be getting any tattoos
i'll give you the drum on that right now

why not i said   with all the
arrogance i could muster

you're just a kid now but you'll
grow up & you might find yr'self
in all sorts of trouble
     you don't know what the future
holds

whadda ya mean i asked

you might rob a bank
     you might kill someone . . .
you don't know what's around the
corner
     so you don't set yourself up
to give the coppers an even break
     get that through your head
now he said

& went back to reading his paper.

Creating a Dilemma

When i think about being sixteen
    i can clearly remember
the exhilaration of being chased
home by a police car late at night

fearless on my BSA 650cc Gold Flash
    sparks flew as i flattened
the bottoms of the chromed mufflers
laying hard into the corners
    to gain more distance on them

my rear vision mirrors vibrating
so wildly there was no clear vision
of their flashing lights
    just enough to see them dropping
back as i'd scream up Hampstead Road
    then kick the bike back through
the gears closing in on Copley Street
    the hollow boxes cackling
    the light switch now flicked off
& i'd squeeze down hard with my right
hand on the front brake
    the telescopic forks dipping deep
under the strain
    knowing i couldn't touch the brake
pedal   its flash of light a dead-set
giveaway

& with my heart in my mouth i'd round
the corner to the left
   gun the bike past eight houses
& make a sharp right before flicking
into the second driveway on the left
   to nuzzle the bike against
the kitchen wall & hit the kill switch

& i'd sit there quietly . . .
   feeling the thump of my heart
slowing inside the lining of my jacket
   waiting on the swissssh of the prowl
car as it flashed past our driveway

knowing the coppers would then face
the dilemma
   should they turn left
or
   should they turn right

& i'd walk inside
   flick on my bedroom light
& see the boy with the Brylcream hair
grinning at me
   from my bedroom mirror.

Changing Gears

Even today   over forty years rush by
at the speed of sound
each time i approach the intersection
of Henley Beach & Tapleys Hill Road

i was stationary at the traffic lights
that particular summer's morning
      sitting on my BSA Gold Flash

a screech of tyres alerted me
      & then the sounds of crushing
metal & shattered glass before
the hiss & rise of steam
      & though mid-morning on a
Saturday
      there came a stillness then
that still spooks me even now

it was the front seat passenger from
the car with the broken windscreen
i saw first
      she looked close to full-term in her
flowery smock
      had both her hands cupped around
her nose
      but even then i was thinking of her
unborn child . . .
until she dropped her hands & i saw

her nose was spliced across the bridge
back to her cheeks

i'd like to say i was an urban hero
    tell you how i kicked the side-stand
out & ran to her aid
    but i was barely sixteen & the flow
of blood terrified me

all i could do was click the gear lever
one-up & let the clutch out quickly
    hell   i've seen plenty of blood
since then –
    much of it my own

i'll never know if she & her unborn baby
made it through safely
    my only hope is they did ...
& that she doesn't remember that day
anywhere near as clearly
    as i still do.

Seasonal Work

In the summer of '66 i was sixteen
& took up a seasonal job as a
steel fixer
    i'd frame up holes in the ground
with reinforcing rods which became
backyard pools around Adelaide

my boss was ten years older
    premature baldness had caused
him to shave his head & everyone
called him Racehead

he called me   Boy

but it was his driving as much as his
head
    that won him his name

he drove a sky blue 1961 Austin
Westminster with a white roof
    it had a 6 cylinder 2.9 litre motor
& four on the floor
    he'd removed the twin SU carbies
& had a manifold built for a four barrel
Holley stolen off a Ford Customline
    & extractors fitted with a sports
exhaust   & the car had been lowered
by two inches

when you hopped in you had to hang on
    even when the 6 x 4 trailer was
attached

one morning we were low-flying along
Montague Road   then a narrow strip
of bitumen with barely a house in sight
    i saw him look into the mirror
& grimace   he jumped on the anchors
& screamed   *we're losing our gear*

we hopped out & watched the 20 litre
white plastic drum which held our tapes
string lines & hand tools rolling
down the road
    but the contents were amazingly
still in the trailer

Boy   he commanded   *jump in the
trailer & sort out that mess
    i'll get a rope from the car*

i climbed in among the bolt cutters
    the heavy guillotine   shovels
long handled spades   clear plastic tubing
    pick   mattock   & crowbar
& was pushing the offcuts of reo bar
to one side to rearrange the load
when i heard a car door slam

& then we were off
Racehead twisting his head around
& grinning like a raving lunatic
as he fishtailed the trailer on & off
the gravel shoulder

i grabbed hold of the rope rail either
side   my knuckles white   the wind
whipping through my hair
grit on my tongue blown up from
the trailer floor   tools bouncing up
& thumping into me   & Racehead
still with his foot flat to the floor
laughing like a madman into the
rear vision mirror
& on it went for another two
or three k's until boredom overtook
him & he drew to a halt

i was glad when winter arrived.

The No-Shame Showman

It was February of 1966 & i was
16 years of age   mid-morning
one Friday   driving my old man
back from a business meeting
　　we were in his EK Holden
travelling north in sunshine along
O'Çonnell Street North Adelaide
　　the old man in the passenger
seat as he'd just been pinched for
drink-driving   again

as we crossed the traffic lights at
Tynte Street he started animatedly
screaming   *pull over/quick smart/*
stop the bloody car/pronto
　　i panicked thinking one of the
wheels might be going to fall off
　　& drew the car to a quick halt
alongside the kerb
　　he was out of the car in a flash
then casually leaned in through
the open window & said
　　i'm going in to the Oxford
for a drink   you'd better come in
with me

you're a bastard   i said

tell me something i don't know
he replied

he was a no-shame showman & when
we breasted the bar
      his hands were shaking like he had
the DT's
      i'll have a double St Agnes with a
drop of ice & a dash of water
      & a schooner of beer . . .
oh   & you'd better pour a lemonade
for my driver

then from his pocket he shakily drew out
a clean folded hanky   flicked it open
& lay it out flat on the bar towel

i was like the barman & had no idea of
what he was doing

he then proceeded to fold the hanky
in half on the diagonal

the barman set the drinks down & called
the tune & the old man   still with the
ducks'n'drakes   pulled out a ten shilling
note & slapped it on the bar   he then
went back to work on the hanky
      first folding the outer point in to the edge
then bringing small folds together until he
had a strap of fabric as wide as his belt

still shaking he carefully picked up both
ends of the hanky with the tips of his fingers
    then ducked his head & quickly flipped
the hanky over the top of his head to rest
on his neck

leaning over the bar he then wrapped his
right hand around the double brandy
    & still shaking & trembling with the hanky
intact   drew down on the fabric with his
left to create a pulley which lifted the glass to
his mouth without causing spillage
    like me   the barman looked on amazed

then without losing a drop he downed the
drink in one swallow & placed the glass back
on the bar
    & the shakes had completely disappeared

he extended both hands in front of himself
for the barman & i to inspect   & to me
    there wasn't a hint of a tremble or shake

jeez i needed that to settle myself he said
    refolding the hanky & casually putting it
back in his pocket

drink up   he said   raising his beer
    we can't muck around here all day . . .
we need to get mobile
    there's work to be done.

Give & Take

It was a typical mid-February
summer night in Maylands
    the corrugated iron roof
creaking & cracking after a 40°C day
    my sister getting close to the
bottom of a bottle of Riesling
    her two grand-daughters
tucked into bed asleep
    her own daughter stacking away
the dinner dishes they'd just
washed & dried
    when they heard the rumble
of a car come up their driveway

looking out the window it was a rare
& unexpected visit from the estranged
husband   father   & grandfather
    a handful of visits over twenty years
along with a lack of any form
of maintenance
    had hardly endeared him

yet here he was   dressed immaculately –
along with his latest blonde bombshell
    both sliding out of his '73 Corvette
Sting Ray convertible   top down
    fire engine red   white lambswool

seat covers & steering wheel cover
    & him taking her hand to lead the way

after the click-clack of high heels
on the front porch it was his daughter
that greeted them
    ushering them through to the
kitchen table where her mother
was seated

well   what a pleasant surprise
said his former bride
    her voice laced with acid
we should have a toast to you both ...
    & just what is this one's name
darling

he perhaps didn't envisage that
the visit would be easy
    but he was brash   & cocky
& flashed a smile ignoring her

to break the impasse his daughter
asked   *how's your mother*

but before a word could tumble from
his lips her mother snapped
    what are you asking about her for –
you haven't seen or heard from her
for over twenty years
    she means nothing

& then he fired back
   & she fired back
& he fired back
   & she fired back
& it was all so reminiscent of twenty
years ago

but he didn't give her a black eye
this time
   just wrestled her out of the
kitchen   along the hallway
& pushed her into her bedroom
   then locked the door

ever resourceful   having survived
with three kids for many years
   she quietly let herself out
of the bedroom window
   & found the garden hose

she was still standing alongside
the driver's door thirty minutes
later
   the hose spraying full pelt ...
the lambswool totally soaked
   & water running up & over
the door sills

goodbye   she said   & left
them to it
   having the courtesy first –
to casually turn off the tap.

Mark & Brian

Even though Mark & Brian were
brothers   they liked to drink
together   & often when they'd
drink together
    they'd fight together

sometimes with one another ...
& other times with other drinkers
    & it might be over a game of pool –
or simply a sideways glance they
didn't like

& when they fought one another
    & others tried to drag them
apart   they'd give them a hiding –
    & go back to drinking together

they drank daily at the Enfield
    the Hampstead
the Northern Tavern   or the O.G.
    wherever they were welcome –
moving from pub to pub when one
of them got barred
    & when they were both barred
from their regular haunts
    they'd front up at the Windmill
or the Windsor Gardens
    or even roll on down the hill

to the Reepham   counting down
the days
   & when three months had passed
they'd be back in with a wink & a nod
   to test their luck   again.

Life at the Bar

Brian   went to the bar
as a young man in the 70s
        fought some hard cases
in some supreme settings
        & won some memorable
decisions

when he first took silk
he was a mild celebrity
        strutting about town
in a tailor-made jacket
        cut for his broad shoulders –
barrel chest & ham bone arms

& he had the patter then . . .
        words as fluid as his lethal
left hook
        as smooth as his silk shirts

but in the early 80s the black dog
bit him   & then it ate his tongue

in the early 90s he had   **G'DAY**
        tattooed across the back of
his neck in thick blue ink
        & he spent days at the bar
reflecting into his pint glass
        not turning to acknowledge
anyone

G'DAY   said it all.

Facing Reality

My four adult children talk
to each other on Facebook

they also talk to their mothers
on Facebook

those of my own children
who have their own children
    tell me that they too all talk
among themselves on Facebook

i don't have Facebook
    i have a blade razor
shoes with laces
    buttons rather than zips
& i talk to my children
    & their children –
by phone
    or face to face
(& let's face it . . .
    sometimes we do talk
about books)

on the phone this morning
my youngest son informed me
his eldest son
    who is now ten –
has girlfriends on Facebook

he said that over the weekend
a girl asked Mason
  if he'd like a bit of lip action
at school on Monday

yes   but where?   was his reply

we can go behind the shelter sheds
at lunchtime
  would you like that?

of course . . .
that's why they call me the love doctor

i'm thinking now
  that maybe –
i am on the wrong page.

Riley

The little man just
turned two
when he hit his first
childhood illness
    chickenpox

& all the little kids
avoided him
    & some of the big kids
too

& he was itchy
    & blistered
& stuck at home with dad
playing with Thomas the Tank
    watching the Wiggles
& scattering the toybox

when nana arrived
    mid-morning on Saturday
she smiled & said
    did Riley have chickenpox ?

no   he replied
    i had bacon & eggs.

Happy Days

We had three sons over
our thirteen years
    & often it was crayfish
& flowers

on the occasion of this
wedding anniversary
our youngest posted:

'Happy Anniversary mum.
Dad said it would be
49 years today!!!! LOL'

she replied:
'And thanks to his infidelity
I didn't have to put up with
him for 49 years.'

our middle son added:
'Crayfish for dinner mum. You
should be celebrating. xx'

our eldest son posted nothing
remained like me
    uncommitted.

Breaking the Famine

I'm a fifth generation Irish Catholic
    my lineage going back to Cornelius Goodfellow
of County Tyrone who arrived on the
Frenchman in 1858
    a year short of a decade of the end
of the 'Great Hunger'

i don't know if any of my forebears
grew potatoes in Wallaroo where they
settled
    but i do know i've lived at the same
address for eighteen years & never grown
a crop of potatoes in the sandy soil
of Semaphore

but the famine will soon be over in my
suburban backyard

the soil is tilled   the fertiliser spread
    & the tubers are growing their short thick
sprouts   spread out in a cardboard carton
in the warmth of my dining room window

in a week or ten days i'll take a sharp knife
    cut those tubers to give me an eye
or two
    & bury them in the furrows of the rich
& ripened soil
    then spread the rows with straw

i'll water them religiously . . .
    & in two or three months
i'll dig them carefully   sparing them
a spear of my four tine garden fork
    & i'll devour the whole crop slowly . . .
mashing them
        boiling them
            roasting them
& i will toast my forbears with every meal.

Little Mister Loudmouth

I don't like to be critical but
but jesus
        christ
               & general jackson
(the three bravest men who ever
left Ireland)
    that eldest hot cross bun
of mine has written a bloody book
about me
    you wouldn't read about it –
well   not unless ya picked up
a copy
    Poems for a Dead Father
he called it
    & the critics have called it
too   the bloody thing got short–
listed for the *Age* Book of the Year
award
    maybe he's not as stupid
as he looks

of course it's all exaggerated
    he always was a bullshit artist –
reckoned i drank too much
    & his mate David Gurry
the magistrate who launched the book
    he backed him on that point too

i'm not gunna run cold & get done
like a dinner though
　　i wanna set the record straight –
i mean a bottle & a half of St Agnes
a day is hardly a drink　is it?
　　most blokes i knocked around with
pulled up after the first aristotle
　　but f'r Christ sake　if you were
still sober after lunch you'd have to go
back to work　i mean fair crack of the whip

still　he didn't shit-can me altogether
　　i mean i liked the launch –
it was a grouse show　a bloody beauty
　　the Coopers was turned on –
that was a nice touch ...
　　worth goin' for in itself
& didn't Mark & Brian go fer it
　　they looked like John Landy
& Herb Elliot when the loudmouth
stepped away from the microphone

half the bastards that should've
been there didn't front though
　　one of the best things about
being dead is that you can just
float around　sight unseen
　　& observe things ...
i like to keep an eye out –
　　Lois looked a bit mystified
by the proceedings

but she's nearly 83 so i shouldn't
say too much
    she had Anne to look after her –
but they looked like they were looking
after each other
    it was good to see the grandkids
smiling
    ah   i'd like to be able to tease
them again
    & the great grandkids too –
by jeez i had some fun with them
when i was sober

no   it wasn't a bad turn-out really
    the back cover blurb said i taught him
love   loyalty   & laughter

i think he got a bit confused though
    probably when he started smoking
all that dope back in the 70s
    i think he got lust   licentiousness
& loudness

to tell the truth it was good to hear
my name barked out again
    someone oughta tell him to
tone it down a bit though
    he needs to pull it back a gear –
little mister loudmouth
    that's what i used to call him . . .
nah   nuthin's really changed.

The Iceman Cometh

Eugene O'Neill may well be dead
    yet still   the iceman cometh

but now it's anarchism & capitalism
    & the misfits roll in on fat Harleys
or in tricked-up black Commodores
with tinted windows & low profile tyres
    the little wheels are going out for
the big wheels
    & now their profiles are being tagged

gold rings glint with crystals from
every finger
    neck chains weigh heavy on heavies
as Noms work hard to push their point
    to move their points –
& it's ten points to the gram

& with every point   they'll tell ya
    they're kicking goals.

True Love

I met him in the education block
at the youth training centre
    he had a mop of blond hair –
dull lifeless eyes   & lay slumped
in his seat like a seal

i've got nuffin ta write about
he mumbled

write about what you're in here for
i suggested

he rolled the puppy fat resting on his
shoulders & said
    it's juss fer robbin a store

you're kidding me son
    how old are you

i'm furteen

& how did all this go down

i wen inta a servo wif a pair
a sizzers & sed
    givvus ya money

but th bloke   he juss laft at me

it made me angry so i fort
i'd try en kill im
    i swung at his froat
but he moved back & i couldn't
get me arm in far enuf
cos of th bars

then i had to back off
    i had ta go fer th door

the coppers got me juss down
th road

i reely didn't no wot i was doin
    i'd been on th ice en booze
fer five days

i juss reely wanna get out now
so i can get back on th ice
    i luv it.

Collateral Damage

When i think about the war
    & Afghanistan –
& collateral damage
    i think about Mark . . .
& his weakness
    (or love)
or his perceived lack of it

& still i count him as a
casualty

shooting away madly for
over twenty years
    his teeth ground down
to blackened stumps

he is forever wounded

as he wounds too

& the battle rages as he
seeks that easy target

there's no white flag –
his sights are set
    the score –
ever so important.

Monologue to a Wayward Niece

Listen Krystal it might well be 28°C
& a lovely sunny day but your aunty
& i don't want you sitting out here
on the front lawn with your home
detention bracelet wrapped around
your ankle. we've put up a two grand
cash surety to keep you out of jail
& we don't want you messing up again.
you can sit out on the back lawn
in the sun but we don't want you out
on display. if one of your old mates
wanders past & offers you a choof on
their ice pipe you'll finish up falling
for the three card trick & failing
your next urine test. then your aunty
& i will have to forfeit our bail money.
so come around the back now. you
know what i mean. i don't want any
arguments & i don't want any dramatics.
now don't go giving me that sullen face.
we're trying to help you as best we can.
we both know that no-one else was
willing to put their hand up again. this
is ya last chance. ya do understand that
          don't ya?

Kleva Voomun

I kleva voomun –
speek five langvij
    Enklish
    Arabic
    Turkish
    Kurdish
    Rushun

mi naem Suheyla
from Baghdad
    but Baghdad
no moor
    Saddam kill mi
if i return   hang mi
    but i luv heer

i goot hellth
    kleva voomun
goot mind –
    i run from Iraq
in March 1991
    i got 3 chouldren
2 gerl   1 boy

i don't vunt mi sun
die for nutheeng
in Amerika voor
    i tell him sun –

to run
    i run with him

everiday i cri
    i'm friitink
i run with doorturs
too
    got no husbund –
that bich man
i don't wun to si
no moor
    he live Amerika –
Chicargo
    i sine for deevoors
long time ago
    1978

i got nutheeng now
    mi doorturs maree
    sun maree
thay lif Germany
    but i lif heer –
Orrstralia

wen i run with chouldren
    Kurdistan
    Turkey
nobodee gif mi wun bred
    kristchun peepul
ar goot
    how thay saa

Grate Britisch
i saa
Grate Orrstralia

i am singool
i am aloan
i am okay.

Chappy

Chappy's nearly sixty
    a nuggetty bloke with
a ruddy complexion & a bulbous
red & purple nose
    Chappy reckons he's the
fittest alcoholic in Port Adelaide

i swim every day of the bloody year
    hardly miss a one –
i won't say i always stay in long
    but i do get in

i reckon that's why i've come good

just before they cut me to get
at the cancer
    the bloody anaesthetist
comes in for a chat

how are you feeling Mister Chapman?
he says

well   how do you reckon –
i'm shittin' myself
    this is the first time i've ever
been cut

you're in good hands Mister Chapman
    try to relax

before we can go into theatre though
i'm going to have to ask you some
personal questions
  are you comfortable with that?

yeah   fire away

now   i will tell you that i do need
honest answers

sweet   i told him

do you smoke cigarettes or
marijuana?

no   i said   *not for over twenty years*

do you drink?   he asked

yes i do   as a matter of fact
  i do like a drink

do you drink much?   he enquired

well yes   i probably do

how much would you drink Mister Chapman?

well . . .
  i have 25 cans on a Monday
  i have 25 cans on a Tuesday
  i have 25 cans on a Wednesday
  i have 25 cans on a Thursday
  i have 25 cans on a Friday

i have 25 cans on a Saturday
& if i'm not feeling too seedy i'll have
25 cans on a Sunday
but to be honest –
sometimes i do have a day off

the doc looked at me squarely
& said
don't worry about a thing
Mister Chapman
we'll have you back on the piss
in a week

& he did.

War Dance

It's 12:20 am when my neighbour
cranks up his stereo & awakens me
    again

this has been going on for nearly
two years
    & i'm grumpy –
i've had more than enough

the police are ineffective
    the landlord doesn't care
& my neighbour thinks he has
a natural right to party

i carry my stereo & speakers
into my bedroom
    flick on the AM band & tune in
to a local Italian radio station
then crank the volume full tilt . . .
    i close my bedroom window
& exit the room
    shutting the door behind me
& muffling the door frame with
my quilt

i drag a mattress & bedding
downstairs
    move into my dining room
& set up a base camp

with the dining room door closed
i'm asleep within minutes

at 2:30 am i'm awoken by my
neighbour   he's stomping over
our corrugated iron roof
    banging his fist into the
iron & yelling & screaming for me
to turn off my music

these are the same standover
tactics i hear him use on his partner
    & she always buckles

after fifteen minutes of not getting
any attention he wearies
    climbs back through his
kitchen window
    & i get back to sleep

at 5:15 am i'm awoken again
    he's doing another rooftop
war dance & banging on my upstairs
window

i ignore his efforts
    & my Italian music plays on

ten minutes later he gives up
& i go back to sleep

at 9:00 am i get up & turn the radio
off
    & after eight hours of Satie
Donizetti   Mancini
& Morricone
    i hope now   *he comprende.*

A Fair Bet

It was 9:07 am & pension day
as i walked past the entrance
to the Federal Hotel
    i was interrupted by the sound
of a wheezy cough
    & the whiff of tobacco

a woman shuffled out of the
the gaming room
    she was somewhere around
fifty
    had on a faded black blouse
skirt & cardigan
    & the creases in her clothes
could only be matched by those
in her tired face   her eyes looked
like they might only come alive
with the sounds of jangling bells
& the sight of flashing lights

i watched her wander across the
main road & enter the supermarket

wondered how her luck was holding
& whether she'd be buying
    steak
        or sausages.

The Ballad of Big Boy

Big Boy had zips over both eyebrows
& teeth-marks across the bridge of his nose
Big Boy's face was a roadmap of ugly red scars
& his right eye was partially closed

Big Boy took it straight from a flagon
from a bottle or from a cask
Big Boy gulped it down like mother's milk
till it dropped him flat on his arse

Big Boy was little more than a baby
just a young buck of twenty-four
Big Boy couldn't resist the lifestyle
temptation's a devil for the poor

Big Boy grew up on a mission
in a house that was hard & rough
Big Boy shaped up as a southpaw
he was always big & mean & tough

Big Boy was a hero for others
the man who could even the score
Big Boy loved to show his courage
he'd often fight two or three or more

Big Boy met his match in a bottle
the one that was wrapped over his head
Big Boy slowed right up after that one
Big Boy became a punching bag instead.

The Ballad of The Magdalene Centre

There's sixty men in the lane tonight
for a chance at a three course meal
you could pick-pocket the lot of them
but there's not a lot to steal

not a lot of money that is
but their wealth's in songs & stories
some of them have lived treasured lives
& tonight they'll relive their glories

there's one man with a broken arm
there's more with a broken heart
there are many running from booze & drugs
there are those who want a fresh start

there's a few who have a girl on their arm
there's more who wear a tattoo
there are some who travel from state to state
there are some you just wished you knew

there's Spiderman from Brisbane
a cobweb spread over his face
a red-back tattooed on his cheekbone
Boggo Road was his disgrace

one man sets down a yellow swag
another parks a shopping trolley
Jay jokes *there's a home on wheels*
there's always humour in human folly

Boozer Karpany plays the spoons
Cedric's on guitar
there are people in a tight circle
Cedric's voice makes him the star

Sharon's just turned twenty-one
has crazy purple hair
shows me tattoos on her upper arms
Grim Reaper gives me a stare

Dustcoat Baree is in uniform
a smile spread over his face
he introduces Uncle Wally
i think both are from outer space

there's two brindle dogs & a white one
they are tied up to a post
there's a punk girl wearing a dog collar
i don't know who scares me the most

one man says   *i get a pension*
another says   *i got hit by a car*
another whispers   *i want pain killers*
while another says   *ta-ta*

John rants & raves about the bible
his voice an endless tape
Bruce says that he will pray for Mark
but he doesn't push the faith

yeah   Bruce says he will pray for Mark
but he doesn't push the faith.

The Knockout Man

When Terry signed the contract
to engage me as his boxing manager
    i believed he could go
all the way

he'd been brought up in a tough suburb
    had gone to a tough school
his father was a veteran of 150 pro bouts
    & was still punching on at fifty
in front bars & hotel car parks after work-
ing as a slaughterman at the abattoirs

i tried to explain to Terry the need
to be worldly
    telling him there was more to life
than just boxing
    & that i'd help to broaden
his skill set

he'd never been to a French restaurant
    so one Saturday night we climbed
the red carpeted steps in Hindley Street
    to be seated by the maitre d'

as we looked over our menus
i pointed out the *cuisses de grenouille*
    & explained they were frog legs
then i pointed to the *escargots*
    & explained they were snails

Terry sat staring at his menu for
some time
    then summoned the waiter –
& with a broad Australian accent
said   *excuse me mate*
do you have frog legs

of course sir

great   now hop out to the kitchen
& tell the chef i want a rump steak
    medium rare

i knew then i was in the company
    of a real knockout champion.

A Light Bulb Moment

I place the object
on the bottom shelf
of my fridge

it is an Iceberg lettuce
    as big & fresh
as a newborn baby's head

two weeks later
it remains unmoved
    & is limp –
& jaundiced

when the light blinks on
    i hear it cry.

A Knowing Look

After i left my second bride
i moved into Room II at the Federal Hotel
    it was less than a rifle shot away
from my former matrimonial home
    & had been described to me
as 'a family room'   which i found
mildly amusing

most days i would pick up my
daughter & we'd spend hours in my
room playing games   reading
stories & poems & nursery rhymes
    singing songs & drawing pictures –
while other days we might go to the
beach or the playground

for the first eight months i spent most
nights alone
    choosing to be celibate

but when that phase passed i brought
back some young women
    while others were not so young –
some of them ex-wives   others –
current brides
    one was a doctor's receptionist
another a meat packer
while one was a former federal policewoman

there was little discrimination ...
   it seemed i'd learned nothing

one night Genevieve left her wine glass
on the bedside table
   when she left to go home to Bob

the next morning my three year old daughter
ran to the bedside table on her arrival
& pointing said
   look daddy   a mummy's glass

only three   & already a poet.

Great Value

I drove into the BP Station in Lorne
      noticing not one signboard
to suggest a per litre price
      & even before i touched the
brake pedal
      i knew i was about to get burnt

but the tank was nearly dry
      & i couldn't see an option

when i re-hung the nozzle
& walked in to pay
      i noticed a bloke who looked
to be the boss stacking shelves with
grocery items

a woman who i think may have been
Chilean
      swept behind the counter to
serve me

congratulations   i said
      as she got close

i beg your pardon   she replied
      with a softly accented voice

congratulations   i repeated

what for   she asked
    raising her eyes to create little
furrows in her brow

you've just sold me the most expensive
fuel i've had to buy on this trip
    156.7 per litre
i think congratulations are in order

she dropped her dark eyes into the
charcoal laminex benchtop
& whispered
    i'm sorry   it is not my fault

hey   i said brightly   *i know that*
    i'm just trying to give you something
interesting to talk to the kids about
at the dinner table tonight

she broke into a wide grin & her dark
eyes shone
    suddenly   at least she –
was great value.

Righting the Wrong

The prison officer in the guardhouse
at Risdon Jail was a big man with
a grey beard

i had to sign-in to go through to
the education block
    & he eyed me with a distinct
curiosity

on my way out i had to sign-out
    & return a numbered lanyard

it was then he seemed keen to
expose his intellect
    & he leaned back in his swivel
chair & said
    my grade five teacher was the
best teacher i ever had
    if we didn't do our writin'
properly we got rapped over the
knuckles
    i've still got beautiful writin' . . .
i'm not a good printer but i've got
really good coercive writin'
    education is important

yes   i replied   *i couldn't agree more*
    coercive writing is very important –
that's what i teach the prisoners.

Don't Look So Glum

Don't look so glum mum
    don't look so glum
was that a finger
or a thumb mum
    don't look so glum

i've been out having fun mum
    yeah out havin' fun
don't poke out your tongue mum
    don't look so glum

my homework is done mum
    stop wavin' y'r gun
all assignments are done mum
    don't look so glum

you're old & i'm young mum
    your best days are done
dad's been gone f'r five years mum
    don't look so glum

yeah i've tattooed my bum mum
    & put a stud through my tongue
it's not the end of the world mum
    don't look so glum

i don't do hard drugs mum
    i go to parties for fun
so get off my case mum
    don't look so glum

sure my skirt's a bit short mum
    but you can't see my bum
don't nag me again mum
    i'm dressed to have fun

i practise safe sex mum
    i'm not particularly dumb
i get love & respect mum
    don't look so glum

it's a mad crazy world mum
    & i need to have fun
year twelve is a drag mum
    three months & it's done
yeah   leave me alone mum
    three months & it's done.

Your Days Are Done

You're such a cad   dad
    you are such a cad
you cheated on mum dad
    & you left us all sad

we lost our nice house   dad
    you made life a drag
we don't like y'r new wife dad
    she thinks she's so rad

we're staying with mum   dad
    we've got a new pad
the weekends are ours dad
    too bad if you're mad

we've got our old friends   dad
    twenty k's is a drag
you can email or phone dad
    it's not all that bad

you've called all the shots   dad
    but now your days are done
your daughter doesn't want you
    & neither does your son
no   your daughter doesn't want you
    & neither does your son.

An Autumn Prune

It is a still autumn morning
    & the sun shines through
wafts of cloud
    a heavy-set man in a black
wheelchair is parked on the footpath
in front of the entrance to
St Margaret's Rehabilitation Hospital

he is catching the morning sun
    & his smile provides some evidence
he's enjoying it
    he is wearing a grey polo shirt
black track pants   & a navy blue sock

his right leg has been pruned midway
between his knee & his ankle
    the stump is bandaged with
a white cloth

he inhales deeply
    & slowly expels tobacco smoke

when he is down to the filter
he rolls his chair back
    drops the smouldering butt
into the SPC Two Fruits can
on top of the fence under the
Smoke-Free Health Service sign
    & wheels his way back through
the electrically operated doors

i wonder how long   this can go on.

Hold On

I'm old enough to remember
the mid-50s
    & Dad pulling into our
driveway in a brand new FJ Holden
    & i can still conjure up
the smell of its pleated upholstery

i remember too   the Green EK
he had when i got my licence
    how he'd let me borrow it
some Saturday nights to take
a girl to the Palais in North Terrace
    & how i'd often climb under
the dash & disconnect the speedo
to help keep him in the dark about
how far i'd really gone with her

& later i bought my own two-tone
EH Special
    Adelaide – Melbourne in $7\frac{1}{2}$ hours
& how i drove 250,000 miles
& barely lifted a spanner

& over the years i've had a Statesman
DeVille and a Statesman Caprice
(of course it's been a long time now
since we've seen a Statesman)

but i do remember seeing the
State Treasurer early one morning
on Semaphore Road
    Kev was climbing out of a silver grey
Mercedes when i stopped and asked
is it true that Holden's are closing?

the announcement will come by the
end of this week   he told me
    you can put money on it

& out at Elizabeth now
    there's no Lion looming over
Philip Highway in Kingswood country
    the Commodore has deserted
the ship
    & there's not a Premier   in sight.

Monologue with the Deputy Principal

Look   twenty years may have
passed & it doesn't matter a damn
whether he'd rolled a five paper
joint   a three paper joint
   or even if he'd put together
a racehorse out of a single Tally-Ho
   there's no dispute as to the fact
they were smoking dope
   & there's no dispute as to the fact
my son had shared the joint with two
girls on the way to the train station
   but it was only him wasn't it –
only him that you bastards knocked
on the head
   three months short of finishing
year twelve
   the girls stayed –
but he had to go   you bastards
yes mate   yes mate   yes mate
   go on   y' tell me now how he's
turned into a nice type of young fellow
   y' tell me now how you were really
impressed after not seeing him for all
these years
   y' tell me now how you are so proud
to count him as one of your ex-students

well mate   i'll tell you now –
    think about what he might be doing
if you & your fascist mates hadn't put
the crunch on him back then
    think about that   **mate.**

At the Violence Forum

He kept repeating
    it's men's business
    it's men's business
    it's men's business
till once again
i could hear the swish
of a frayed electric cord
cut the air
    & over it –
my mate's mother
on the boil again
& screaming
    you'll get this jug cord
her bosomed figure bouncing
across the short-cropped lawn

& he kept repeating
    it's men's business
    it's men's business
till i could hear
that teacher's voice
telling me of her first job
    & the indelible imprint
it left
    his mother had pressed
a steam iron to his cheek

& he kept repeating
   it's men's business
till i saw flashbacks
from a video
shown that morning
   a woman butchered
by a man
   her scars coming out
in waves

it's our business.

A Negative Experience

I'd been in bed alone for hours
    it was closing in on midnight
& the heat was unrelenting

i became alert to the rattle
& scrape of a sash window moving
in my second bedroom

i slipped my shorts back on
    tip-toed towards the noise
& flicked on the light

he was about twenty-seven
    a meth head wearing black track
pants   black singlet   & a red
baseball cap

we went at it hard & fast
    i concentrated on his left eyebrow
until it hung open like a tin of tomatoes
& the white wardrobe was flecked with claret
when i man-handled him downstairs

as we passed in the hospital corridor
an hour later
    him handcuffed to a barouche –
he looked across & said
    you hit hard for an old man

shaddup   i snarled
     or i'll open up y'r other eye

a week later
     my Hep C test came back negative.

Softly but Firmly

I had on a dark pinstripe
merino suit
    black pointy toe'd shoes –
a crisp white shirt
    & a dusky pink tie

i was going to a memorial
service for a former Supreme
Court Judge who was also a
noted communist
    & the tie seemed vaguely
appropriate

the day was cold with sporadic
bursts of sunshine & sudden
showers
    so i wore my black fedora
& carried a black mans' bag

i had time to kill & stopped at
Lucia's for a bowl of minestrone

there was an outside table
    so i took off my fedora
& placed it on the table top

as i opened my bag to withdraw
some money i noticed two men
lounging at the adjoining table

both were in their early thirties –
heavy-set working men
    jeans
    check shirts
    longish hair & facial stubble

i locked eyes with the man closest
to me as he spoke
    he drawled
have you got a pistola in that bag?

i lay the bag alongside the fedora
    took two paces toward him –
& grim faced
    leaned into him as i pushed his
head back with my eyes

i spoke softly but firmly
do you want the barrel down your mouth?

i've picked the wrong man he replied

the soup was delicious.

Life with Jayden

At the youth training centre
fourteen-year-old Jayden sat still
for forty minutes
    transfixed
through my poetry performance

an hour later in the writing workshop
    he kept rocking back & forth
in his chair

stop rocking   i said
    look at me Jayden
i want you to focus
    slow down mate
give me your attention

he stopped momentarily & said
    i thought the poetry would be
boring
    but you talked about family
violence   & how some women
get belted forty times before they leave
    my mum's been belted twenty times
she's had fourteen notifications made to
Child Protection for violence & abuse

i live with me dad now 'cos they finally
split

mum & dad are both drug addicts
they've been on Buprenorphine
for twenty years
mum sells a bit of grass to help
pay the bills & dad can't work 'cos
his back's stuffed

& me dad   he'll swallow anything . . .
purple pills   orange pills   green pills
yellow pills   he just doesn't care

before i went to live with dad
i saw him put a shotgun to mum's face

c'mon   pull the trigger   she said

but he just smashed the barrel
across her forehead
then jammed the barrel in her mouth

& then it was over

mum had a bong
dad sat in the bedroom

& two hours later
they were talking again.

The Family Business

In some circles Ron might be
referred to as an entrepreneur
    a young man readying himself
to take over the family business

the old original family name ...
    equally well known in the south –
& the north
    the cops know it
the judiciary know it
    petty crims know it
meth heads know it
    & now Ron is readying himself
to claim a piece of the action

he's still a teenager
    not a big bloke but nuggety
& cocky
    self-assured with plenty of known
back-up
    & keen as mustard to trade off
the old family name

he's used the colours of his indigenous
flag
    had number 13 tattooed in bold
tri-coloured numerals high over his left
cheekbone
    just under his unblinking eye

& as he has marked out his face
    he has marked out his fate

now
    he's marking out his territory.

School Heroes

There'd been fifty-seven random
phone calls over three months
    teenage boys harassing me
at odd hours with blocked numbers

after the third call i took a punt
& accused the caller of being a
student at a certain Adelaide college

he ignored my guess   pinched
his nose again   then snorted
    GET FUCKED GEOFF
& courageous as ever   hung up

i decided to ignore future calls
    no-one was saying anything
clever   engaging or entertaining
    so i let the fifth call go to
voice mail

an hour later when i checked it . . .
the nasal voice snarled
    I HOPE YOU DIE OF CANCER

having had cancer in 2008
    & again in 2012   & diagnosed
again just two weeks earlier
    i couldn't dismiss that proposition –
& it angered me   not just the words

but the harsh reality they may well
ring true

& they kept trying to torture me
      the gutless gang were at least
persistent
TAKEN YOUR TABLETS GEOFF...
      GET FUCKED GEOFF...
& i kept telling them to stop pinching
their noses
      & that it was only a matter of time
before they'd come unstuck & we'd
meet face-to-face
      & i told them i'd had a trace
put on my line   i gave them every
opportunity to stop

& it did take fifty-eight calls
      but at 1:52 am on the 10th of October 2019
maybe they were a little tired
when they forgot to block their number

once confronted ...
Jayden was adamant that he didn't make
that cancer call
      but he was quick to blame Alister ...
& when neither Jayden nor Alister
would admit to making that call
      i suggested it may have to become
a police matter

straight away Jayden blurted out
IT WAS COLBIAN
    IT WAS COLBIAN WHO SAID IT

at the next meeting with Colbian
    his mother & the Principal
the denials continued
    his mother said she had just had
a double mastectomy
    she assured me her son wouldn't
make a joke about cancer
    she said his dad was badly affected
by a stroke & her son would never make
jokes around health issues

i never did take the 'Cadbury Favourites'
Colbian offered when he finally buckled
& his tears flowed

i didn't want chocolates
    i was just there for the truth.

Brian John Goodfellow
Born Adelaide, November 15th, 1957

Loved youngest son of Lois & John (dec.), loving brother to Annette, Geoff & Mark (Bluey). Loved husband of Janet & loving & proud father of Angus, Joanne, Graham, Tess & Kate. For Brian, life has been a battle. Former Featherweight Champion of S.A. 1973, Lightweight Champion 1974, 1975 & 1976. Awarded the '1973 City of Adelaide Championship Medallion' by the Corporation of the City of Adelaide in association with the South Australian Olympic Council. Brian was also a three times winner of the 'Boxer of the Year' award. Tragically threw in the towel on Friday 24th June, 2005. He'll be missed.

Poem for Brian

Brian   it's the day after
& i've just sent out the above
email to some of your friends

you'll note i've used a boxing
metaphor   along with a bit
of alliteration
        said you *tragically threw in
the towel*
        i thought you'd like me to
phrase it that way
        though i've never known you
to ever dog a blue

(unlike my good self)   & i say that
somewhat blushingly

my first thought was to use
another boxing metaphor & say
     you'd slipped from the stool
but in context i considered it too
literal
     too much an overstatement

overstatement or understatement
     that's the sort of detail
i'm looking for when drafting
a poem Brian   or crafting a poem –
     & craft is possibly the word
most people would use to best
describe a lot of your work

like cutting mitres to fit a set
of architraves
     & doing the job properly –
so you'd never squeeze
a cigarette paper in the joint
     the way you'd do it –
or   had   done   it
     is what we'll have to say
from here on in

it's that fine attention to detail
that you knew so well

you may have noticed i'm switching
from boxing to building now
    but you'll understand that too –
you were a champion at both

but getting back to that
overstatement/understatement
business Brian
    it's about finding balance

you had it beautifully in the ring
    & the records prove it

but as for your public & private life
through the past twenty odd years
    you've been spinning in circles

now   you're back in control.

The Punter

i.m. Mark Walter Goodfellow 'Bluey' died 21st March 2013

Blue was a White Ox man
    dead at sixty
jack dancer of the nanny goat
    none of us overly
surprised
    it could equally have been
cirrhosis of the liver
    & anyway –
an autopsy may have well
proven it was neck & neck

i remember the first time i saw
Blue have a whack
    Noel & Linda tying his arm off
in the shed at Copley Street
    they didn't see me that night
in my rubber soled shoes
    insulated from that shit –
& anyway
    they were all too busy & self
absorbed
    & i slipped away into the
darkness . . .
    silently   & unannounced

Blue slipped away into the darkness too
    thirty-five years later

though he'd slipped away on the
gear a few times too
he was in his twenties then –
but he woke up & gave the shit away

i can't see the romance in it really
it turns my guts to think of
the ulcer he had in the crook of his
left arm
though he generally wore his
flanny shirts   sleeve down
in those days

over his last six months
he still went up to the TAB
as often as he could
he knew the odds were
stacked against him when they
finally got his diagnosis right
he didn't seem to care though –
always on the lookout for a long-shot
he just kept on   with the punt.

After He Stopped

i.m. Brian John Goodfellow 15/11/1957 – 24/06/2005

My late brother Brian lived
in the inner-northern suburbs
    where it was well known he
liked a drink

& it would be an understatement
to say he could be a bit intolerant
    & easily annoyed by fools

& there were times he was barred
from a handful of pubs on the Northern
side of town

it seemed Brian was always thirsty

a couple of days after he stopped
drinking i made arrangements
for his burial

how would you like to dress him
    i was asked in solemn tones –
would you like to bring in some clothes?

we'll bury him naked   i replied

i was given the raised eyebrows until
i remarked   *that way he won't be able
to sneak out for a drink*

as you wish Sir   & i happened to mention
then that i hadn't been knighted
   but it slipped straight over his head

a few days after his funeral i met his
mad mate Mark at his local
   he'd been on the phone to me
crying   & i didn't quite know
how to console him

he'll never be back   he gasped
crying into his 10 am pint
   i've lost me best drinking mate

it was then i opened up & told him
i'd buried Brian naked
   so he couldn't come back
& join him

that stopped his tears
   & i can still hear his laughter.

Like Now

i.m. Heather l'Anson
29th December 1942 – 2nd February 2019

It's just a few minutes past
11:00 am on a Friday morning
    that time when people can
be seen making their way back
to work
    brushing cake crumbs
from their suits & dresses
    catching their reflections
in shop windows & adjusting
their clothes & smiles
    buzzing on double expressos
soy lattes   Irish breakfast
    or perhaps the day's conquests

it's quiet in this room
    but i can still hear traffic
rumbling along Semaphore Road

we are here to farewell one
of our own
    we won't see Heather's image
reflected again
    not unless it's in print ...
she's taken off
    deserted us
she's gone to the other side

Heather was always a mystery
woman
     she'd sit at Semaphore cafes
in summer sun wearing dark glasses
reading the newspaper
     a white cane & her kelpie Zita
keeping her company
     but she was always taking in
more than just newsprint

no-one she knew   would get past her

here he is she'd say
     gee i love those red Speedos
they're just great
     but there were other times i reckon
Heather would have rather seen me
without them

like those Friday afternoons when she'd
tap her cane past Lucias at the Market
     she'd spot me & stop to say
gee i love those red shoes
     they are bloody beautiful

then as quick as she arrived
     she'd be gone

like now.

A Message from Leone

i.m Leone Bernhard, 11th July, 2018

Look at ya selves ya bunch of cunts
   the only reason you've turned up
today was cos ya thought the fucken
will was gunna be read
   well i've got fucken news for you ...
youse are all right out of luck

had a look in the box have ya?
ya fucken sticky beaks
   i left instructions for some poor
bastard to Spackle me up
   i hope i haven't disappointed youse
too much

i see they've put ten handles on the box
   yeah   ive put on a bit of fucken weight
but youse can all get fucked
   it's none of your fucken business

i was keen to go in the end
   got to the stage where i couldn't
tie me own fucken laces let alone unscrew
the top off a bottle of Johnnie Walker
   thank Christ for casks

yeah   it's been seventeen years since
Jackie Boy left me
    fucken hard darts without a staunch
drinking partner
    it's been fucken near ten years since
i could get the cork out of a bottle of
Moet on me pat
    Jackie was a bloody beauty . . .
he couldn't fight for shit but scared
the fucken daylights out of a heap of em
when he pulled out his squirter

half the cunts that shoulda been here
today have beaten me to the grave
    where's Judy Moran?
oh yeah   fucken sloughed up & couldn't
get a fucken black dress & a leave pass
    & Graham Kinniburgh . . .
poor darling . . .
he woulda been here except for that fucken
rat Carl Williams
    well he got his right whack in the end . . .
they all do i spose

well youse can scrub my number out of
your Teledex ya bunch of cunts
    & don't worry about me . . .
i'm not scared of fire.

At Dave's 60th

Even though i'd arrived solo
& ten minutes early
    there were a handful of
other blokes also in their sixties
standing around on the patio

Dave's latest Tinder date was
exiting the family room wearing
a filmy voile party dress
    drink in one hand–
cigarette in the other
    & behind her was Big Norm
the ex-Warrant Officer who'd
flown in from Hobart for his old
mate's party
    if he'd started giving orders
most sensible people would've obeyed

most other blokes were standing
around solo
    & then a few turned up with
their second wife or younger girlfriend
    but others came through
the gate with just an esky in hand

i was chatting to a couple of Roofers
    one had been a ruckman
the other a rover
    & i was looking for a wingman –
anxious to get a lead

we'd been chatting about the perils
of marriage
    standing around as we were
less than a stone's throw from my
former matrimonial home
    it was then a grey haired woman
in her mid-sixties jumped in on our
conversation

the ruckman asked her how she was
connected
    she said *i'm a ring-in …*
there has to be a ring-in at every party
    but the ruckman tapped her again
you must know someone to be here
    she swivelled around like she was
doing The Twist
    pointed out Big Norm
the bloke over there with the grey hair …
    i'm his Tinder date

i knew then i couldn't swipe left
    or right

it was time for me   to move on.

It's Really the New Fifty

For Chris Kourakis, 17th June 2018

& now that you've actually turned sixty
you can really start to count down
the final ten of handling the hammer ...
& there is no infelicitous intent Chief
in reminding you of that dateline
so i won't bang on about that but will
suggest when you do step out of Chambers
& waltz down Gouger to Lucias for lunch
you may occasionally glance someone
who does look somewhat vaguely familiar
in a passing shop window ...
& you might then shake your head
but you won't be on your own entirely ...
other friends will be facing those visions too
& on those family get togethers when you
slip off your comfy shoes when it becomes
your turn to back up to the white doorframe
& have the new pencil mark made under the
ruler you'll start to become accustomed to
the fact that the lines are now moving down
rather than up (it'll be a bit like your libido
really) but soon you will find yourself on the up
at maybe 1 am & 3 am & 5 am to tiptoe quietly
to the toilet for a pee while you try not to
disturb Jane or the kids
& it won't be long before the kids will be starting

to think about having their own kids
    so stay nimble man ...
keep on with the exercise & swimming program
not to mention that Greek dancing style you've
perfected so well but be careful with the Ouzo
so you can well manage getting down on your
hands & knees before retirement does kick in ...
& anyway you'll likely find yourself beginning to
retire a little bit earlier each night from now on
but you'll be rising earlier too (though not in ways
you might like to) but rather to begin the task of
writing those judgements that keep backing up
& you may well find that you'll begin to have
issues too with backing up (& no there are no
toilet jokes) i'm reflecting on other issues ...
like in the driveway & dimly lit car parks
when you can't quite seem to be able to swivel
your head around quite the way you used to –
& soon you'll swear it was your father looking
at you in the mirror through your morning shave
& as for the hairdresser you'll start to find
more time now to visit him or her but it may well
be for your ears your eyebrows & your nostrils
but don't let me invoke concern ...
my intention is not to create a scare or worry you
it's just that i've stayed nine years in front of you
thus far ...
& maybe   just maybe
i'm simply comparing apples   with pears.

A Smooth Number

I'm in my mid-sixties now
    && though memory is such
an imperfect thing
    i do remember listening
to jazz back in 1955

it was likely on the ABC
    the fat valves glowing orange
on the big brown bakelite Blaupunkt
blaring in my father's backyard shed

the old man introducing me to
Miles perhaps
    or was it John Coltrane ...
perhaps even he wouldn't have known
on that particular Saturday afternoon –
    him   more than halfway down
the label on a bottle of Royal Purple Para
port   dancing over wood-shavings
scattered across the concrete floor
around his work bench
    resting the gunmetal handplane
to catch his breath –
&& top up his Vegemite glass once again
    while he rolled his big blue eyes
&& lit another Camel plain && slurred
    those notes are just as smooth
as this red cedar i'm planing.

The Smile

I was in the chemist shop to collect
four scripts

as i opened my wallet
        a tax receipt from a restaurant
fluttered to the floor

i sighed   eyed it momentarily
        thinking of the pain in my hips
& lower back
        & just as i started to squat
a female voice said   *i'll get it for you*

i was already on the move
& mumbled   *it's okay i've got it*
        & scrabbled it up from the carpet

as i stood up our eyes met
        she was around ten years older
at least ten kilos heavier
        & was squinting at me
through glasses thicker than mine

we both smiled

i swiped my debit card
        got another receipt
grabbed my medications
        & got out of there pronto.

A Fresh Start

I've floated around Port Adelaide
for over half a century now
    but never swum in its polluted
river
    rather   i've drifted around
in pleasure craft
    raced around its streets on
motor bikes & rolled around
in cars & trucks   to run out of luck
at times & be pinched by local coppers
for being a lead-foot

i've seen my late brother go from
deck boy to able seaman
    delivered & collected him
from the *Accolade*   the *Troubridge*
& the *Mary Holyman*
    but that was when we had
a working port & ships were
tied up bow to stern
    when men slung baling hooks
& shouldered sacks
    when wharf sheds weren't arcades
of tourist shops
    & the smell of perspiration
hung heavy with summer's heat
    when the sheds hummed with the

voices of blokes hungry to make an earn
    & game enough to use their bodies
as a forklift

i've seen men who once stood six foot tall
reduced to a jockey's height
    watched them wandering St Vincent St . . .
humping their way home to a corrugated
iron shack in Ethelton & waiting on their
disability pension to be approved
    those men are gone now –
long gone . . .
    & the street remains as empty as their
pockets were
    but i'm old enough to remember
seeing the pain they carried in their
eyes
    & i know those men would likely
cry if they spotted Newport Quays today
    the sugar wharf just like them –
long gone . . .
    replaced by a string of white boxes –
but there was nothing sweet for any man
in the weight of a bag of sugar

through the 60s & 70s
i'd often pick my brother up from
The Globe or *The Exchange*
    in those days men stood shoulder-to–
shoulder   pint glasses in hand

while the boots stood in the cellar
tapping kegs & sneaking schooners
        & the blokes upstairs kept a hankie
in each pocket
        one to blow their nose with ...
& the other to wrap their falsies in
just in case some mug pulled on a blue

& in that era when the summer months
came on & the wool came off
        the wool season would kick in ...
& with it came the casual work
        it was eight until eight most days & nights
at Bennett & Fisher   & Elders
        their jarrah floors creaking with weight
& slippery with lanoline
        & when the season finished if you were
desperate enough you could slip over to
the fertiliser works & get a start lumping
bags
        the itch working its way down the back
of your shirt as a constant reminder

the inner harbour's empty now
        the wool stores too –
& over at the fertiliser plant a conveyor belt
& technology have displaced most of the men
        & though the old Ice Works have closed down –
there are men & women trading in ice daily
regardless of the season

the old meth drinkers are long gone –
& a huge number of pubs remain shuttered
& cobwebbed
    those pubs still trading are mostly empty –
apart from pensioners being slowly syphoned
by the dropping of the dollar
    & while the queues form up at Centrelink
the legal aid crowd suck on cigarettes & spin
their stories of bravado outside the court
while they wait on their name to be called
    & everyone except the government
talk in low voices
    about getting   a fresh start.

Strung out in Semaphore

In the streets of my suburb
    two or three men grouped up
in suits & ties usually means
the demons are set to swoop

in the streets of my suburb –
most men if they're lucky enough
to have a job   wear a blue singlet
    shorts   & a hi-vis shirt
unless of course they're fronting
the magistrates court
    or turning up for another
bloody funeral

in the streets of my suburb
    more young women than men
have decorated their bodies with
colourful tattoos
    they stroll comfortably
among the old established locals
    & exchange smiles

in the streets of my suburb
    there are spreads of large hostels –
they are populated by manic depressives
    schizophrenics
mood swingers
& others with acquired brain injuries

many adding colour
& some giving voice to anyone
who might listen
    on these boulevards of broken dreams

in the streets of my suburb
    poverty & affluence –
sickness & good health
surround you
    & at the outside cafe tables
along Semaphore Road
    AFL footballers sip lattes
while a handball away   bin jockeys
gouge for refundables
    & just around the corner
a low hum buzzes
off the high tension wires
    stretched out & strung out –
along Military Road.

Cab Driver's Monologue

You ring fer a cab mate
  yeah jump in mate –
don't worry about the beer
drink it in the cab mate –
doesn't worry me mate
  'cept i'm jealous

Semaphore eh
  used to live down Semi
meself
  full of lezzos & weirdos
but don't get me wrong
  it's still a great place

i'll be havin' a beer or two or three
or more in about an hour when
i knock this fuckin' job on the head

she goes alright with a bit of a kick
in the guts eh
  don't mind speedin' a bit
do y' mate
  fuckin' times i've sped
down this road mate
  know every fuckin' radar trap
the bastards set up
  hate fuckin' coppers mate
& i know a shit load of 'em too

yeah   i'm an Ambo mate –
just drive this bastard fer me
beer money

yes mate   i've pulled 'em
out of cars wrapped 'round poles
on both sides of this track
that house over there mate
    the one with the pine trees –
junkies mate
    Narcan'd a bloke there
a couple of weeks back
    & fuck me if i didn't do his sheila
three days later
    Narcan'd her i mean –
too skinny to fuck mate
    you'd be rockin' on the bone

that one   the one with the white
Commodore on the front lawn
    pulled a stiff out of that joint
one night
    old cunt   he'd just curled up
& died   looked like a fat millipede
when we shovelled him up mate
    been there fer about two
fuckin' weeks
    newspapers all over the joint –
& fuck mate   did it stink

i was with Big Bruce that night
　　they don't call him Big Bruce
fer nuthin' either
　　i'll give y' the mail –
the big fella loves his beer
　　drink both of us under the table
i'll give y' the drum
　　& not too shy to have a slab
in the back of the ambulance
of a hot night either
　　mmmmmmm　we put away a few
that night
we've put a few away on many
a night me & Big Brucey
　　beer & bodies

now that joint mate　the one with
the long grass　rental joint
　　got a call there the other
night　or mornin' anyway –
it was about two-thirty
& cold as a nun's cunt　& mate
　　every fuckin' light in the joint
must have been turned on
　　looked like Torrens Island –
i didn't toot
　　the fuckin' music was blarin'
so i flashed me lights
　　no cunt came out so stupid here

has to bang & holler at the front
door
    now i'm no racist mate but this
blackfella comes out & pokes a fifty
in me snout & tells me he wants
a packet of Holidays
a two litre Coke
& a large special pizza with the lot
    mate   did i tell him to get
fucked quietly
    i give him a nice bake

orrrrrr   that one is it   i'll swing
around   this one here eh . . .
yeah   seventeen will do it
    thanks mate   keep it eh –
sweet
    most cunts don't tip these
days   don't even wanna talk to y'
    you're a gentleman   a dead-set
gentleman
    best end of the day is a west end
of a day
    orrrrrrr   Coopers is it
doesn't matter a fuck does it?
    a beer's a fuckin' beer mate –
have a good one
    goodnight mate.

A Cardinal Sin

I'd best describe myself
today
 as a submarine catholic
but sixty years ago
 well after my baptism
 my first holy communion
& my confirmation
 i would have likely said –
practising catholic

most friday nights back then
i'd find myself with Father
 kneeling before him
on the carpeted step of the
confessional box
 my little red face
pressed upwards to the grille

& even with that flimsy black
fabric shrouding the grille
 i knew that he knew
who i was
 as much as he knew
that i knew who he was
& after he'd dissolved a few
easy one's like *i swore*
 (he never asked what
particular words i'd used)

& after i'd admitted
i've been rude to my mother
 (he never asked what
my behaviour had been)

& after i'd mumbled
i missed mass last sunday
 (he never asked
if i'd been to mid-week mass)

but always after i'd told him
i've had obscene thoughts again
 he questioned me at length –
& lingered over this . . .
 wanting to know each
& every detail

& by george
 i think i've finally
worked out why.

Cardinal Trucking Responds

Appearing at the Royal Commission via video link from Rome, Cardinal Pell likened the Catholic Church's responsibility for child abuse to that of a 'trucking company'. If a driver sexually assaulted a passenger they picked up along the way, he said, 'I don't think it appropriate for the ... leadership of that company to be held responsible.'

By george   he said
i've grounded our entire
fleet of drivers nationwide
i've told the blokes to loosen
their collars for a week
there's been some problems
with the blokes not being able to
pull up   but i'm onto it –
that's my job

as an outfit we're responding
we're trying to rectify our
faults
no organisation is perfect –
we've all got our limitations
we know all too well we've
had this problem with pulling up
but as i said earlier –
i'm onto it & i'm responding

we are about to check the brakes
on all our drivers
 the main brake   (to be sure)
but we're going to check the
hand brake too
 & i'm committed to ensure
we have an emergency brake
 there'll be no exhaust brakes –
they are obviously too noisy
 & we like to keep things quiet

now   if you'll please excuse me
 i've got work to do.

Dark Shadow

It is the 25th May 2015 & Cardinal Pell
features in an ABC online news article

the story reveals how Pell visited his
old school   St Patrick's College in
Ballarat about two months earlier

today   there are calls for him
to re-appear in Ballarat at the
Royal Commission Into Institutional
Responses to Child Abuse

allegations have been put he tried
to bribe the nephew of a paedophile
priest into staying quiet about his abuse

the photo accompanying the article
was snapped by AAP photographer
Dan Himbrechts
       it recorded Pell's departure from his
appearance at the Sydney Commission
in March 2014

the photo reveals Pell in a crisp white
shirt & black jacket
       he is seated in the passenger seat
of a car wearing a seat belt
       he is looking pensively into the lens
of Dan's camera

there is a dark shadow over the top
of his head
when i close the news article
    what i remember best ...
is that dark shadow.

Photograph: Dan Himbrechts

Existence is Suffering

She told me on our first date
she was a Buddhist

i commented that as a teenager
i'd always worn ripple sole shoes
    i said it gave the ants
a fifty – fifty chance

she laughed & said something
about the fact that i was funny

we laughed together for about
five years
    but by then my jokes were
getting a bit like the arse of my
Levi jeans
    & soon our smiles turned
into snarls

& i wasn't up   for the dukkah.

An Old Flame

I kept a box of tea
light candles in my
bedroom

they had a two hour
limit

i'd light one when she
arrived

when the flame went out
so did she.

Different Approaches

Fast approaching the blowing out of
seventy candles i'm walking the beach
at Semaphore
    chasing the 10,000 daily steps
that might provide me greater longevity

at the water's edge a middle-aged man
kicks a small beach ball into the sea . . .
& his black Labrador retrieves it

the dog drops the ball on the shoreline
but the man has walked on & beckons
the dog to bring him the ball

the dog remains motionless
    & the man re-traces his steps

this scene is repeated yet again

i begin to laugh out loud but hear
the sound of my father's voice
    absent now for twenty-two years

i recognise i have my father's sense
of humour
    but my father only married once
& he loved a drink

his head was often leaning over
the front bar of a range of city
& suburban pubs

my head was often buried between
the legs of a woman in a range of city
& suburban bedrooms

both of us
    as stubborn   as that dog.

Home from Hospital

I lie in the foetal position
in my double bed
    & though 4 kg lighter
following pneumonia –
find my spot in the nest

after seven days away
    i keep waiting on my
bedroom door to open
& hear a nurse state
    i'm here to do your obs

unsettled …

i roll onto my left side
    my tinnitis follows.

Possibilities

For Katy

When the specialist physician
explained my test results
i started to panic
    our eyes locked in the
bleak silence of her room

when she did speak again
she stated
    there are two possibilities

the most likely diagnosis sounded a real
mouthful
    & i couldn't understand the jumble
of words   & asked her to repeat it
    twice

yet still i couldn't take it in

what does it mean?   i asked

she said it was a mild form of cancer
    that someone my age would not
generally be taken by it
    that it needed perhaps 20 years
to fully develop
    & other causes of death were far more
likely

i was slumped in my chair   slack-jawed
    trying to make sense of it . . .
& gaining some courage
    asked about the second option

that   she said   *will take you quickly*
    but i don't think you need to worry

it was far too late for that though –
    having spent four & a half years cheating
death from throat cancer –
    i wasn't keen on another battle

i asked her to write down the two
possibilities
    & she filled the page of an A4
Clinical Record Sheet
in bold cursive letters with a black biro

Monoclonal Gammopathy of Uncertain Significance
&
Myeloma

& slid it across her desk

it was a warm morning in early December
yet i felt numb
    i picked up the sheet of paper –
rose to my feet & said
Merry Christmas   in my cheeriest voice

Merry Christmas   she replied
    & she rose   stepped around
her desk   & hugged me

it was then   i really started to worry.

The Pressure Is On

We appear as four spacemen in our
clear plastic hoods
 but we are out-patients aged sixty
plus –
men with white plastic collars
wide as dinner plates around our necks
 each inset with a blue latex grommet
trimmed for our individual necks
to create an airtight seal for the hoods
which rise hand-high above our heads

cancer & radiation have brought us
together in this hyperbaric chamber
 two of us recovering from
head & neck cancer –
 & two with prostate –
blood flow & our inability for wounds
to heal naturally our new enemies

two corrugated plastic tubes
hook up to the base of our dinner plates
to feed us
 we are now ten metres below
sea level breathing 100% pure oxygen
in this recompression chamber
 expelling air through our exhaust
pipes

our location is a cross between a
shipping container   & a submarine
     all metal   with five portholes
a hand span wide –

at times an outside operator's
eyes will peer in on us
     though we are observed close hand
at all times by our intensive care nurse
in her bottle green smock & pants
     she adjusts equipment & removes
our hoods for the five minute break
on the hour
     & serves us water & tea & coffee & biscuits
which arrive through an airlock cylinder

& whilst she is ever present we are all
monitored on CCTV   & no chances are taken
with a night vision camera as a back-up
should power fail
     & she appears fail-proof with a
torch at hand

we spacemen wear a regulation uniform
of cotton tee shirt & track pants
in contrasting navy blue & grey
with blue surgical bootees over our socks
     there are no watches
     no iPods
     no phones
nothing that could cause a spark

we sit quietly in our sky-blue vinyl
recliners
    the floor is a matching blue with
a non-slip sparkle & the walls & ceiling
arctic white
    a blue console cabinet around three
walls shroud the supply & exhaust pipes –
the mixed air supply & the suction
supply   we all seem to have the blues

Charles fills his two hours by solving
Sudoku   & when beaten or bored
reads *Le Gloire de mon Père*
    Mick works through a Dick Francis
novel
    & Arthur has a pink Texta in hand
to slash lines through a book of
Sudoku
    yet we all remain puzzled about our
respective conditions

i am scheduled for thirty sessions while
others are set for forty
    & we are all at different stages of
treatment

our nurse is seated in a beige vinyl lounge
chair as we time travel
    all of us wanting to look at a watch
or clock ...

& while she receives instructions through an
earphone   & converses with the doctor
& operators outside
     her booteed feet are propped up on the
stainless steel hand basin
     i note she's three quarter way through
reading the novel *Fourth Day*
     this reminds me i am now on day seven

from my armchair i see small orange lights
through a porthole
     they flash on & off in a control panel
three metres away
     i listen to the constant hiss of air being
pumped   it sounds much like a 70s air-con
overpowered at times by momentary
mechanical clanging & clanking which
stops me from dozing

the walls around us are scattered with
brass & metal valves
     many have splashes of red & green paint
to indicate supply & exhaust
     but there are switches too   & hoses
& couplings & gauges & filters & dials & i feel
lost among this gadgetry
     & for two hours   until the airlock
access door clangs open
     the pressure is on.

Preparing for Business

Stretched out on the operating table
in a white gown
    i looked up & around the room
at the faces of the surgeon
& his trainee
    the two anaesthetists
& several theatre nurses
    all preparing for business

to break my nervousness
    i said to the nearest nurse
geez it's cold in here

i'll get you a blanket she said
    & she wrapped me like
a baby

don't worry about the cold
she confided
    it's always like an icebox in here

why is that?   i enquired

it's to keep the doctors awake
    she whispered.

Acknowledgements

Some of these poems have been broadcast, recorded, or otherwise been published in print in the following journals or newspapers.

ABC 891 on-air broadcast with Ian Henschke, Antipodes (USA), *Best Australian Poems* 2014 and 2015, *Big Issue, Canberra Times, Eureka Street, Family Matters* (India), *Homeland, Offset, Saltlick Quarterly*, 'Songs of the Street' CD tracks 2 and 11, The Collective of St Mary Magdalene & Studio Masters Adelaide, *Tasmanian Times, The Adelaide Review, The People's Poet Transformed, The Saturday Age, Violence: Directions for Australia*, Wangaratta Jazz Festival Postcard Series by Extempore.

Geoff Goodfellow Annual Postcard Series x 1,000 in 2015, 2,000 in 2017, 2,000 in 2018, 5,000 in 2019 and 5,000 in 2020.

Geoff is also indebted to the South Australian Supreme Court, District Criminal Court and various Magistrates Courts for displaying 'Monologue to a Wayward Niece' as framed A1 posters inside court complexes. Also thanks go to the Tasmanian Supreme Court for the display in their Criminal Court Foyer and to the Ipswich (Queensland) Court Complex which have supported this initiative.

My thanks go to Geoff Page who advised me extensively on the original manuscript, but ultimately the final choice has been mine.

Bouquets to Michael Bollen and the crew at Wakefield Press for their continued support, advice and encouragement.

A special thankyou to Simon Cecere for his cover photograph and author photo.

Out of Copley Street: a working-class boyhood
Geoff Goodfellow

This playful, tender, richly realised childhood memoir – his first prose collection – reveals the vulnerable side of the working-class boy from Copley Street. Growing up in Adelaide's inner-northern suburbs, Geoff inherits a quick mind and quicksilver tongue from his father, a tender but troubled war veteran (and talented glassblower) who struggled with alcoholism. Geoff's dad teaches him to make things with his hands, staunch loyalty to family, to charm and cajole – and perhaps most enduringly, to tell stories.

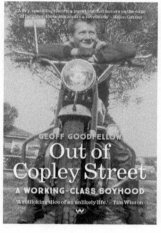

So we follow young Geoff as he takes his first job as a milkman's assistant, aged five, fixes up his first motorbike aged eleven, flirts with housewives (and punches out his boss for insulting his dad) in his first job as an apprentice butcher aged fifteen, and hitchhikes to Mount Gambier to work on oil rigs aged seventeen.

This is a poignant snapshot of working-class Australian life in the 1950s and 60s, expertly rendered with the vivid lived detail and wry knockabout humour that Geoff Goodfellow is famous for.

For more information please visit www.wakefieldpress.com.au

www.geoffgoodfellow.com

Printed in Australia
AUHW020757200221
341505AU00004B/4